Living on Madison Avenue

ഔ ∞

David Lawrence

FUTURECYCLE PRESS
www.futurecycle.org

Cover photo by Philip Maier; author photo by Marisol Cifuentes; cover and interior book design by Diane Kistner; Cronos Pro text and titling with Impact

Library of Congress Control Number: 2018946026

Published by FutureCycle Press
Athens, Georgia, USA

ISBN 978-1-942371-55-7

*To my wife, Lauren, who helped me
to discover myself in loving her.*

Contents

Prose on the Fringe of Poetry

Drowning in Poetry

Prose on the Fringe of Poetry

Brain Snatcher

I passed the green light of go only to run into the red light of stop. At twenty-two I was high on mescaline and couldn't tell whether the red light meant go or stop.

I could have been run over but a friend advised me how to skip past cars. I thought he was teasing when he said that red meant go but he didn't actually say that as I wasn't hearing too straight.

I don't know why my generation thought that it was cool to get high. What makes me human is my fabulous consciousness, not my escape into confusion and stupidity.

I saw Timothy Leary at Bethesda fountain in Central Park. He looked like a nice man but was a monster who wanted to devour our consciousness. He was a brain snatcher.

I should have celebrated being high on clarity. I should have worn reality like designer glasses. I should have appreciated what I had rather than what I neglected.

I am the genie who escaped the bottle and discovered that I could sit on the bottle cap and look over my own signature terrain.

Still Crazy

When I was sixteen my mom sent me to the shrink because I threatened to kill myself. I hadn't thought of how because I didn't really mean it. It was just a way of getting some sympathy and getting out of my responsibilities at school. It was a way of being a cracked egg instead of one that was hard-boiled.

Oh, it was fun to think that I might be crazy. I felt superior to the sane varsity kids in their do-good sweaters.

When Vietnam came around I was called in for a physical. I convinced the army doctor that I was crazy. Like I had to be crazy to avoid getting my legs shot off. Like I was nuts to love life. Like I was inferior for recognizing that war is real and for keeps and I wanted to keep what I had—my legs, my arms, my lips, my brain.

In jail I convinced the shrink that I was manic-depressive. I don't know why or how. He gave me some lithium. I threw it in the garbage.

When I got out after two years I felt messed up and went to a shrink who said that I was manic-depressive. He also put me on lithium. I have been on it for fifteen years and love my wife like a peaceful piece of rye bread, like a bland snack. As the homeboys say, she is butter baby.

I've had a lot of experience with semi-craziness. It makes me feel important. I like feeling different. I like the possibility that the mental institution is right around the corner when it isn't.

Label me whatever you want. The labels don't stick to me. I am not short pants in a camper's valise.

All My Little Candies

I wanted to throw myself down a hole and shovel dirt on my head when my dad died last week. Tears strutted around my eyes like an emotional dominatrix in fishnet stockings, a leather thong and a whip. I punched myself in the head for the fun of pain. I transferred money from one pocket to the other; I paid for my hurt, for my disconnect, for my dad's dying.

It's precisely one week later. Sunday morning. I meet my old high school friend, Marc, for coffee. He apologizes for my dad's dying before I say it. He has a nose for death. His wife died five months ago in her sixties. My father's death is not as large as his wife's death. It is a small private thing; almost all of us hitchhike on the fading bodies of dominant shadows.

I feel a little less sad confronted by the enormity of Marc's wife's death. We are at that age where dying is as noticeable as a season; autumn, perhaps. I better get used to the collection of unhappiness in a dish like little candies.

Passing loved ones are sweet. I unwrap their little colored tinfoil and pop their deaths into my mouth. Delicious, I love them all, all my little candies made out of memories and chocolate.

It's Not Friendship

There are times when the fog rolls in like a log. I am as loud as the invisible is quiet and as congested as a cough that is stuck in your friendship. Oh, it's not friendship. It is love. It is unpredictable and fated to hate and softness to anger and entreaty. I am in love. For years I didn't face it. I hid from feeling close to you like a gopher gone into a hole. I hit my head with rocks so I could have lumpy thoughts. I walked off into enmity like a hot foot with a match in the soul. And now I'm back to say that I don't understand the belittling of lightening into a spark and the diminishment of friction into caresses after dark under the light of your intelligent eyes. Love is the absence of definition in the emotion of intent vagueness. I am you receiving my kinetic need as I identify with what you don't do when you foretell the inexplicable.

Eat Up

So you gave a lot and then a little and then there was nothing left to
bring home in your doggie bag from your dinner with me.

So I munched on the disappearing scraps,
kissed you like you meant it
and tried to resurrect your indifference
into a splash of passion.

It's not that I feel your indifference but I feel that it is sometimes there
like an abscess in a tooth or absence from a grammar school class.

I need what you're not offering but I know that you haven't completely
taken it away; it's just that your attention isn't locked in on me when you
cast a sideways glance at my fish in the pond.

Thanks for staying in the neighborhood of my friendly persuasion like a
movie screen that has dropped down on my head.

Is that popcorn or your teeth
cracking on my fingers
as you try to bite into the knuckles and meat
of our relationship?

Accident on Madison Avenue

The doorman, Fred, tells me that two women on the corner are trapped under a car. He looks frightened. I didn't know that he cared about anything but the door—what goes in, what goes out and what goes around.

I step outside. The corner is surrounded by people and ambulances. I can't get a glance at injustice's wheels. I do not even hear the screams. What's happened to "I scream, you scream for ice cream?" I recognize their silence. Death shouts are caught in their throats.

A mummy queen is lifted over the crowd on her stretcher. She is passed about like a serious artifact. She is valued for her suffering. She is an obelisk of pain.

I don't want to be a Peeping Tom at death's elevator foyer. We are in the land of the marbleized rich. Madison Avenue is a clumsy place to die.

I go back in to my doorway and tell Fred I couldn't see much. "It's what you don't see that appropriates the result," he says.

He didn't really say that. He is not that smart.

I go upstairs. I wait for my wife to wake up to brag to her about the accident I had almost witnessed, the collision with things I shouldn't do and mishaps that are simultaneous with failed efforts.

Reading Your Book

You are welcome even though you don't thank me. Welcome always to
find companionship in the flip of a penny or love in the unwinding of
winding emotions.

That's that
and the indigo of the sunrise
is veritable
ink.

Ask a squid?
It is written in his philosophical squirt.

I am glad that you came my way when there were so many other routes
open to your embrace. Closeness is at the end of the trail but also along
the route in the dune grass.

So much integrity in the failure
to open up the book of your emotions
which I read
through the spine like braille.

Living this life has been a magnificent rise into borrowed branches
as I and the leaves reach up to the sun-friendly sky above the pause
of trees.

One Eyeball

Sometimes the feelings throw themselves across the felt like dice. You win or lose but it doesn't mean that craps is a no-brainer.

The girl that hangs from the trampoline is my wife in my naked imagination. We are swinging to the accordion of conjugal pressing. The music is our consistency, our eternal sound.

I never knew that there would be no other women in the world. They disappeared into my obsession with getting it right with you.

You let me hang from your braid. You don't have a braid. That's why your permission is so eye to eye.

We are seeing through one eyeball. Or is it a marble, something thrown from the thumb into a pack of glass?

Divorce is yesterday's news, the sixties mistake. Time we found togetherness in a pillow on a couch in our museum. We get one shot at the target. And we pull the trigger again and again.

Trees

The log that fell into the river went for a long swim into a hidden country where logs were the dominant culture and the trees wept as they saw their barky cousins floating home.

My wife loves trees
and cries
when a branch breaks on 72nd Street.

I don't care whether trees come and go like soldiers in formation and lie down like the wounded in a futile war.

My wife likes plants too.
She puts an orchid on the windowsill.
I bought it for her for Mother's Day.
She is not my mother.
I want her to be happy.

When we walk down Madison Avenue to the St. Regis Hotel for our Sunday tea sandwiches, I will pretend that I am a tree and hold her with my leafy hand like we are nature's thrill.

In an Idle Comment

I was getting C's in all my courses in Great Neck North High School.
I didn't really know it. The only time I worried about my report card
was when I brought it home. I don't know if my parents really cared.
One time I dropped the card in a puddle and changed the grades.
Not much. A "B" here or there. It didn't matter. Or I don't remember
that it did matter. My parents didn't seem to care much about grades.
I don't know why. They were rich. My dad had done well. I was neither
here nor there, an afterthought, a grade on someone else's paper.
In my senior year I ran into Jimmy Cogell in the hallway. I hardly knew
him but he said, "You're not as stupid as everyone thinks." I was shocked,
appalled, awakened. I suddenly realized the image I was presenting of
myself as a dummy. I didn't want to be what I seemed. I was popular.
I dropped all my friends and started to study five hours a day. I got
mostly A's straight through my Ph.D. Cogell who was nothing to me
changed me from a failure to a high-grade aficionado. He was my
inspiration. For the next decade I'd bring home my grades to my parents
and they celebrated. They deserved it. They were there for me even
when they weren't and they let the sunrise of the day unfold itself on
the beach of tomorrow. I was a crab. I nitpicked the waves with my
claws. I studied so hard that I had to wear glasses. Failure was my
inspiration. I found myself in Cogell's idle comment. I did not need
a good school. I needed a good comment.

A Career of Sorts

I have chewed tobacco for *Men's Fitness* magazine. A modeling job that made me vomit.

I did a commercial with Anna Kornikova. They dressed me in a gorilla suit and she hit tennis balls at me. No one ever saw me. I was the suit.

I was the subway bum on all the posters on the trains for seven years.

I was a Smith Barney investor in a convertible with Donna Mills in *Town and Country Magazine.*

I was an ex-millionaire who was out of jail two years and was looking for a new career like a pair of binoculars looking for its focus on a bikini on the beach.

I never quite made it. I did something that never arrived. The shadow of nothing kept slipping my footing out from under me.

I fell at your feet and asked you to take me back. That was twenty years ago. I want to thank you. I am thanking you.

When I die I will hold my hand out so that I can lead you from earth to whatever. I will invent heaven so that you don't have to deal with nothingness in a failed universe.

Intentionality

"I have proof that God exists," my wife tells me on the telephone. She explains that when God creates the mouth, he does so with the intention of teeth, so that we can chew, so that we can survive. To her it is all about intentionality. I say that I don't think God cares if we survive. He kills us all in the end.

She tells me that I am Darwinian and that I think everything is by accident. I tell her that if God were great he wouldn't have created mouths; he wouldn't have given us the need to eat; he wouldn't have left us hungry as I am hungry for her kiss.

"You're a jerk," she says, then adds, "What about the eye? It's perfect." I tell her that I don't think it sees far enough and that if God created it, it would see forever in the night."

She hangs up. I really want to tell her that I believe in God but I don't. She is afraid I won't go to heaven with her if I don't accept Christ as my savior. I'm not sure why she wants me around her in the next world; she always seems a little frustrated by my company here on earth.

Dillon

You fought Meldrick Taylor, Julio Cesar Chavez, Ricky Haddon and
all the usual suspects. Now you're a trainer at Gleason's Gym. Me too.
I never fought those guys. I wasn't that good. Although I did fight
on Chavez's card at the Mirage Hotel in Las Vegas. I'm proud of that.
That's a big deal to 99.9 percent of the population. I could blow myself
up and float at the Macy's Thanksgiving Day Parade. To you, if it's not
the main event it's nothing. As a fighter I was an oddity, out of place,
too old, not particularly good. As a trainer I am a philosopher, more
interested in telling my students about life and how to look into
absence and find meaning. I want to educate everyone and discover
what's missing in the holes of my life. I am learning. I am teaching. I am
the outside invitation into finding the dubious meaning of being here.
I've had to go through a lot to get nowhere and appreciate the rotundity
of zero, the luxury of a cipher.

Sleeping in Separate Rooms

When I am in bed at night I sometimes think that I have a knife. In ninth grade Michael Heffernan stabbed himself in the leg.

I only remember the dramatic. He sliced into my mnemonic heart. Memory bleeds. It is a piece of itself handed off to future reminiscence.

I think of when I first knew that I would kiss you. It was after our lips met like strangers in the night. You told me that your favorite movie was *Idiot's Delight*. Where is Frank Sinatra in all this? I did it my way. I was a straight A student.

Even though I don't have a knife in my bed I stab myself with the thought that you are in the next room sleeping. It is forty-three years after. Remember the band, "Ten Years After"? That was chicken feed. We are the proof that marriage is the residue of consistent love. We go on *ad infinitum* like a marathon.

I could go into your room and wake you but you'd be startled by my senior indiscretion. Your name is Lauren. It wasn't popular when I met you. I love you like closed shades. I am involved in the interior of your house.

If I slept in your bed I would only wake up to piss every few hours and disturb your figure skates. You don't like company when you are preparing to be evermore. And it's good for me to get used to the loneliness of eternity in a handful of pillow down.

The raven quoth the startle of the beyond and then goes on some more in the tuck of the invisible after-all.

What We Mean

Sometimes I twist my thoughts up like twine. I am cat's paws picking
at myself. I am what sticks to the confusion and what frays like wool.
I am your everlasting love in a fork on the road where we were supposed
to go straight through to sanity. But we are insane. We are not. If I just
give up we will have a picnic lunch beneath the trees and throw lilies
on the pond. I love you as much as I hate myself. If you pass the wine
I will break the bottle on my head and show you that I am willing to
bleed for you. Like you should care? What doesn't matter makes a big
difference and I find I would marry you over and over like two spools
rolling down a hill in summer's diversion. I don't mean anything that
I say. I am its product. I am its meaning.

My Tooth

It almost fell out. I pressed my tongue against it and Joshua felt the wall come tumbling down. I didn't fight the Battle of Jericho. I licked myself, defeated the absence of an enemy, and felt my tooth go askew.

I dig a grave for my youth. There are worms in my inspirations. There are broken hands holding empty glasses. These breathless failures sneak up on me like a gravestone with sneakers. I look behind me and trip over the lettering. Here lies "David Lawrence," a pinch of aspiration in an ambition of failure. There is hurt in a bottle and sadness in the cork.

I call my new dentist. The answering machine tells me he and his cronies are busy. The disorientation of ambition. Taking on more than he can chew, chomping his teeth like dancing marionettes.

It seems my new dentist can't even afford a good secretary. I do not want to be treated by a recording. I do not want to face the irreverent reversal of service in the black cape of extraction. Death be not proud; be John Donne, be a dentist. Go away. Pull your own roots.

I will try to stay calm. If this tooth falls out I will be walking around with a space in my mouth like Halloween. I will be haunted with the ugliness of old men trying to bite a pear with mushy gums. I remember the loudmouth lack of bites in jail. A thousand threats for every stabbing.

A nickel for a molar. The tooth fairy is in the shower blowing the drag queen. I am sickened by all things that decay and perversion renamed by the overly humane as a fine set of bicuspids.

Doing My Own Thing

There are recondite nuances in the wind whose explications are willow heads. All this meaning nothing except that beauty is its own surmise, guess, circumference.

That word you almost said
is as beautiful
as your lips

saying nothing,
being precautionary,
unintentionally secretive.

I love you like my prescription for lithium. You keep me in balance when the weights are falling off the shelves and the balloons are flying away with my first editions.

All around me the flowers are attacking winter. I like a good snow.
I like being cool. I like wearing snowshoes in the absence of color.

A Ski Life

I look up into the sun and see my shoes. I am standing on my head.
I am a coin that can't flip onto tails. I am Bosco in a glass of milk in 1959.

When I went to ski racing camp at Mt. Rainier I thought I was an adult.
I was a kid. Not a goat. I wanted to be in the Olympics but although
I was good I was not good enough by a long shot, a rough glacier, an
irrelevant remark.

I didn't know what girls were. I used to arm wrestle with the female
cook, Mary. Nice Catholic name. She was from Maine. No one could
beat her. I didn't recognize that she had other parts besides her strong
wrists. If I had, she would have been more threatening.

I wrote postcards to my mother and let her know that I was a mountain.
You couldn't get me down. I was my support, my boulders, my ski slopes
above the tree line. I thought I would die in the mountains. I liked the
idea of becoming a snowdrift.

But life turns on itself like snow in a gust. I look around and I haven't
skied in twenty years. My life of snow has fallen from me like a drift
dumped by a plow.

I don't ski anymore. I don't know where to address my postcards
to my mother. Do they ski in heaven? She never liked it much. I guess
you feel that way when you're not good at something. I don't know.
When I'm not good at something I quit so fast that I never get to feel
the disappointment.

Cuts

When I punched myself in the face I meant it. I really tried hard.
I could afford to do moderate damage. But when I took out the razor
blades I was timid. I didn't dig in deeply to my cheek. I scratched it like
a butterfly of blood hovering over a gardenia. I don't even know what
a gardenia is. I don't care what most things are or are not. I am two steps
away from reality and hiking into my own world like the start of a
continuous game. It's not that it never ends but that the finish line is
the beginning of a new ending. I do a dance in the end zone. I don't even
know where that is. I don't like football. I am un-American. I move in my
own circles like I am balancing on Jupiter's obscure rings. I know a Jew
who went to an anti-Zionist meeting. He is a self-hater. I told his brother
that I am a Jewish anti-Semite because of him. I can't stand my own
people siding with their enemies in order to feel broad-minded.
My wife calls these left-wing liberals "Jump-in-the-oven Jews." If he
were a Moslem speaking out against the Palestinians they would have
used my razors to decapitate him. They know how to stick together,
to coagulate.

We

Sometimes I wake up in my office and I don't know where I am. I get a
little scared like a cube of awareness thrown on a gambler's craps table.

I'm a bit crazy like that
if you know what I mean
which you don't
but I don't care because you
don't exist.

I think I am sleepwalking and trip over my own feet even though I am
only on my back wondering who I am and why I am here.

Where am I when you are sleeping?
I hope I am hugging you
in your dreams
like a hallucination of lips.

We are dancing together in a disappearing act like silhouettes of
tomorrow in a stretched-out yawn.

It's good to be with you.
You pull me out of the ocean like a breath that hasn't drowned.

I Don't Mind

Sometimes my mind runs down the block ahead of me. I have the choice whether to follow it or let it go. I don't really choose. It just happens. I either race to get it back or turn the other way into unawareness and the simpleminded flow of thought negation.

I don't like to think. I like when thought thinks me up and I am the result of turning the other way and letting the wall slam into me.

Without a mind I am the instinct of a Jungian archetype. I am the history of the nature of my nation like a peanut in a corrugated shell.

You think I am stupid. I don't mind because I have given up my brain and I am the result of the last ice cube that melted in a plastic tray when it was carried in a hot car on a vacation.

I enter the sadness of not knowing who I am and fall in love with Lauren to try to reconstruct myself in her gazing at me. I am looking at her looking at me and find a way to recapture who I was before I lost my way in the forest without trees under weather that was irascible as winter.

Drowning in Poetry

Minor Chords

There is a chipmunk running on the subway tracks.
I know that it is a rat but I want to make the tunnel bucolic.

I call the train a bull.
I paint a sun on the vaulted ceiling.

I see the grisly women in their raincoats as maidens in fields.

A man spits and I say that it is raining.

A pedophile bumps into a little girl and I say that
he didn't mean it,
that he was trying to cover her from the other dangers.

I see a poster of me as a bum on the subway walls.
Not really.
They took it down two years ago.
I got paid five grand for that modeling gig.

I am the light coming out of the tunnel.
I am the underground talent that never fully passed the platform.

I Am a Tripod

A sneeze in the carrot is worth two in the patch.
I am sick with self-loathing.
I can't seem to do anything right after
a history of accomplishment,
a dire draw full of diplomas and the swan song
of a career's wings.
So I come to this:
a patina of failure on a jewel of shortness
of breath.
I lean on your infanticide to understand
modern women and their right to choose
their children's death.
I am walking with a cane.
I can't tell if I have three feet or I am aided
by the spiritual revelation of wood.
I am a tripod.
I have three opinions on all your deregulations.

Strangling a Sherpa

The end glows like a cigarette on my forearm.
        I am burning up.
                I am forgotten smoke.

You pass like a balsa wood glider
and return like a cramp.

You see these things in my eyes and I see
my eyes in your mood reflections.

The last time we climbed Everest
I knew that I could do anything with you.
        But I couldn't.
                I was a rock in Central Park.

I strangled a Sherpa to show that I was mean.
The mountain goats that weren't there were afraid.

Elephant Skin Wallet

When I walk down the street I am outside of my body
looking at my strut.
I catch the glint of my footsteps
and the skip of my heel.
I am part of the traffic
and a little bit of the pedestrian spittle.
I want to introduce myself to strangers
but there is nothing stranger
than me
getting to know my aimless wander and the bounce
of bumping into people.
The people are old and rich on Madison Avenue.
I like the image of wallets floating in and out of doors.
Mine is elephant skin.
It lifts its trunk.
At sixty-seven years old I don't have much to anticipate.
I step on a quarter and realize that I have about one fourth
of my life left to trample.

Riding Madison

I used to walk down Madison Avenue with a saddle.
I was riding wealth.

I was lassoing the vaulted smile of arrogant success
and wrestling it to my kind of ground,
pinned and startling in the faces of homeless despair.

Oh, so happy to be me now
and to have done all that I have done from
riches
to celebrity
to education beyond repair in the ruins
of my poetic nonsense.

And yet I stumble on possible happiness like
a misplaced toe.
I am stubbed.

I have failed in places I didn't know existed and lost
money like a metaphysical wreck.
I am disconsolate in a counter behind the draperies
in a rich shop like Tom Ford's.

The two years I spent in jail were rich.
I counted the coins of my introspection.
I was alone in a group of failures.
I was so glad not to be on death row where appeals
are rampant.

Everyone wants to live, whether or not in a cell.
To live incarcerated is a misunderstood delight.
It is so much better than execution.
I fell in love with myself again in that dormitory for losers.

The custom-made shoes in the window on my street
make we wonder
about the meaning of five thousand dollars and of life.

Nothing

I stick a spoon into my ear and pull out some sounds.
I taste them.
The noise of the brain is delicious.
I had been thinking about thought and heard the gears squeak.
If I had a fork instead of a spoon I would have spilled gin.
When I was young I used to drink until I passed out.
Unconsciousness has its own particular sound—nothing.
Nothing is not a sound.
It is a predilection for the absence of death's presence.

Can't Get Away

It's hard shaking the dead loose.
Is my father grabbing on to my hands or am I pulling
at his cuffs?

When the rabbi asked if I wanted to look at his face
I shook my head from side to side.
I couldn't do it.
I had looked at my grandmother's face in her coffin
fifty years ago
and I still see her disappearing into a vase
like a dead flower.

I can't get over watching my dad's bleached coffin slide
into the pit.
He was short even before he got sick.
He shrunk, littler.
He must have been sliding side to side in the box
like a hapless, pithed toad.

Man, he's got a nice smile in the picture on my desk.
Maybe he's not hurting.
Maybe it's only me who suffers pain.
No relief:
just the raggedness of lonely feelings like the tattered
cuffs of life's rejections.

Ribbons

The things you let go return with ribbons on them,
gifts,
bounties,
unrecognizable mugs from old shots.

You can't get rid of the past until the past jumps
on your shoulders like a dog
and licks your neck,
breathes on your stiffness.

I am the part of your past that keeps unfolding into the future.
I hope that you will carry me a long way.

We are so mixed up like a bundle of laundry.
My sleeve is in your remembrance and we lie down like snow.

Timing

Time is flow and flow is time.
Time out—
I am arguing with the moon when
the sun is still out.
These pictures belong in a museum
but they haven't been painted yet.
I am obliged to you like a favor on loan.
I know the meaning of your cold shoulder
and I put hot fudge on it.
You'll get used to me after we are dead.
It's the loop of time that hangs us from the roof.

Thinking About You

Sometime I am rubber to the road and others I am the road
smeared on by rubber.
I love you like a cat loves its stealthy look and the arch
in its back.
When I come home tonight I'd love to have sex with you.
That's some shit to think about your wife.
But I do love you like the urge loves its quintessence.
I am so mixed up with you that I forget my name.
I am the Mr. or the Mrs. in the couple.
I am married to your impression of me
and soul-mated to your misinterpretation of how I love you.
I guess forty years of marriage is the first step into the tundra
with snowshoes on.
The next step is the naughtiness of a kiss in your ear as I die.

On Stealing Hemingway's Wives

I have the sad eyes of a puppy yearning for his bone.
My face is more sensitive than Hemingway's.
I didn't realize that I was good looking
until I no longer looked so good—in my sixties.
My sentence structure is ephemeral,
wounded,
more beautiful than Ernest's.
He makes much of his manhood.
I take mine lightly.
If we were in the same weight class I could knock
him out early in the first round.
He couldn't take one game from me in a set in tennis.
I could get down a slalom course in half of his time.
If I could turn mediocrity into fame,
like he did,
all his wives would be chasing after me as the *Sun
Also Rises.*

The Skate Key

If you fall on your head your heels will have a good view of the moon.
You will be one of the lucky ones who will not
have a meteor land on her head.
You will comb bubble gum out of your hair
and pretend that you are a little girl.
The hula hoop stops at your hips.
Your roller blades tilt into your toe.
I didn't know you then but I would have wanted the skate key
to your heart.
You are yesterday's outreach into the blinders of tomorrow.
I am an atheist who is inventing heaven just to have a place
to sip tea with you after we are gone.

In Your Birdcage

If I go walking in Central Park I will pull down the shades
of the sky,
cover my nonchalance in blue,
apologize to the squirrels for stealing their acorns.
Oh one big happy skip and a jump.
I am highly happy.
I am up and away in my mysterious balloon.
I am somersaulting through the grass
in deep,
in an erstwhile relationship with my wayward heart and
the woman I have loved like salt over my shoulder,
Lauren.
I will not fly.
I will be married in your birdcage forever with one foot
on the food pellets and night on its way, falling
like the contents in the spaces of a Magritte painting.

It's a Wonderful Life

I fell into your lap like an eye into an awkward view of angels.
    Clarence was there dancing on the head of a pin
with Jimmy Stewart.

It's a wonderful life when everything goes wrong
and you rise above the losses like the head of an ice-cream cone,
            so delicious,
suave and cool like a lick of vanilla.

I come to you with an absence note signed by my dead mother.
Look who's absent now.

When I needed her she was there like April on our front lawn
in East Meadow.

Suburbs know how to comfort the stretched heart.
        I will miss her until I die.
            Then my son will miss me.

He has almost already forgotten his grandmother.
        Don't worry Mom,
I am there holding you above your grave by your shoulders.

Face Painting

I send you a present in a blue box.

Then it is in the past.

You have already forgotten the joy you felt
upon opening it.

It's as if the present never existed.

Maybe it didn't.

Maybe I sent you an empty blue box
and you painted your face with the sadness.

From the Other Side of the Totem Pole

Beautiful is as beautiful doesn't which stands outside itself
Like an aroma around a pear.

It is who you are when I see you from a different slant,
a glance knocking itself against your improbabilities like
a rubber ball on a window.

I slide down you like cognitive dissent,
a relocation of my past attitudes towards you into a new place.

And you become fabulous like the first time I met you
in the Hunter College cafeteria and knew that one day I would find

your carved beauty looking at me from the other side
of the totem pole.

Grandstanding

Walking past all the ugliness in the world I run into you
at the beautiful corner and know that you are the glow
beyond the traffic light.

You are so unusual that I stop and go and watch
you shift gears as you smoke into my universe like
a runaway wheel.

You are so Daytona lovely.

I want to get into a major accident with your chassis,
to roll over with you into the injured audience.
I want to share your accidental drama in the grandstands.

You Got Me Babe

I patted one side of my head and snow fell out the other ear.

When I'm thinking about my youth,
     about skiing,
          it is always winter.

I liked turning fast past trees so that I could almost die
like Sonny Bono.

I could say to the frozen universe, "You got me babe."

There is something warm about a blanket of cold snow.
I snuggle up in a drift and go to sleep for twenty-four hours.
     When I wake up I am a new day.
Perhaps even a new month.

I am the snowstorm that you don't see outside your window.

I am the season that forgot to change because I am in love
with the way frost bites when it is hungry for your company.

Leafy Sky

The sun looks like a vegetable in a patch of blue.
I am the stalk.

I am the connection between everything
foreign
and all that is underground.

There is a spade in my handshake;
I turn you around like a potato.

I steal an aquarium from your living room.
There are fish on the lawn.

I want to put you in a net
and dip you in the ocean like a crab.

I want to wave to you like you are a cruise boat
taking off from shore.

There is a distance between us
that makes us tread the nervous laps of water
on borrowed pontoons.

Dog Story

I've been working on this all day long.
It is almost finished.

I don't know what it is because its face
is turned into itself.

A mouth is biting into its nose.

The dog is barking in the neighbor's backyard.
It confuses its leg with a bone.

I never ran over a dog.
I'm curious.

Would I feel the fuzzy feeling of guilt or
the malignant glow of a killer at the wheel?

Thinking About It

The more I see you the more I want to be you so that love
becomes self-identity and I am what I admire in the haunted house
where ghosts indicate possible boutonnieres.
Time passes,
passing closes

and what arrives must leave before it comes back
in a quandary of introspection.

If there were answers to the absence of questions
we would arrive at conclusions that we were never meant to espouse.

I know we could love for a hundred years if permanence
weren't interfered with by the vacillation of death in igloos.

I Am Not Lunch

I jump on my head like it's a diving board.
I am wearing swim fins.

There are sharks in the pool.
    I kick up to a star
even though it is not shining in the afternoon.

I wave at the sharks
        arrogantly
                snottily
reminding them that I am not lunch.

I talk to Tinker Bell on the North Star
and she tells me not to grow up and if I believe,
well, it will all be well.

I don't really give a damn but I tell her "I do"
because I don't want to hurt her feelings.
I am that kind of guy.

I think politeness shines and truth is a rude
        distraction.
Life is a tea party with manners and filters.
Who cares if we ever get to drink the tea?

The Kid on the Subway

An ethnic of some sort offers me his seat on the subway.
    He is in his teens.
            Do I look that bad?

I can do fifty chin-ups and beat down a so-so boxer.
I am handsome, I tell you.

I see the girls looking when I shyly look the other way.
    So what's up kid?
You want a granddad to beat you down?

I know you're just being nice
but I haven't died and come back with sod on my head.

I am not the about-to-be-forgotten.
I am not yesterday's news haunting the subway.
    I am here to tell you...
Oh, what's the difference?

It doesn't matter if I trip over my own tongue in a senior
ballet of balance.

At the next stop the kid gets up from his seat.
    A reprieve,
he was getting up anyway so his offering me his seat
was no insult.

He wasn't feeling sorry for an old man.
He was just getting ready to be on his way.
    I feel a little better.
I don't kick him in the butt as he leaves.

Spooning

I take out my eye and put it in a spoon.
It is a soft-boiled egg.

I eat my vision and it becomes insight.

I see the landscape inside myself and know
that I am part of the trees and the shrubs.

I am a psychological arboretum.
        I bought a ticket.
                I am a tourist.

I take fertilizer from my pockets and feed
        the plants.
                I am God.
I am responsible for someone else's garden.

Endless Passage

The bullet goes through you and out the other side.
You are a shot-up thing.

Little darling,
it's hard to watch you bleed on the veranda
beneath the waiters delivering their cocktails.

You are holy like the Catholic Church
or Swiss cheese.
You are lactose intolerant.

You feel the wounds like life's accidents.

You try to fill the holes with denial but just end up
bleeding into death's affirmation.

Life is an artificial interruption in our endless passage.

Green House

You don't want to freeze the hose in the summer
because meltdown is in the grass.

I ride a butterfly over your delicate pajamas
and go to sleep with you in the green house.

We plant ourselves in vases
and make of ourselves bouquets to the glass-refracted sun.

We sell ourselves to tourist life
and become part of the recreation of stragglers.

We are an arboretum of colorful pansy emotions.
Let the sun play on the scratches of our roof glass.

Head Bump

The temptation is not the attraction but the removal.
As you are moving away I am going towards you,
banging my head on your magnet,
lost in your crazy maze.
If I hang onto your sleeve it is because I want to be
garmented by you.
I want to be the button on your cuff.
I want to be your tomorrow in your today and your today
in my tomorrow.
It all doesn't make sense or dollars.
I am the cost of doing marriage with a marginal mind.
As long as you pay the price I will sell myself to your advantage.
We never know which way we are going when we bump heads
or don't.

Niagara Falls

If I died a thousand deaths I'd at least like to die one for you.
    Maybe all of them.

I am so involved with you that I feel like I am your skeleton.
I give you structure.

You give me a handle to hang onto in a waterfall.
    I am Niagara Falls.
I am hiding in a barrel as I fall onto a tourist boat.
    I am smashed.

I have drunk too much emotion.
The water is vodka and I am getting high on tasteless waves.

I am holding onto an admittance ticket to the park.

I don't belong here when I am thinking about you
and more serious matters up near the Canadian border.

A Brazen Hug

I am a critter.
I am all fuzzy and affectionate like an apology
     after a breakup.

I come to you like tummy rub or a brazen hug.

You want your critter.
     Your critter wants you.

There's something supernatural about me.

I guess it's the way I circle around you like
     a flying saucer.
All my Martians have a crush on you.

We are taking the same trip among undiscovered
planets.

We are in La-La Land among unidentified emotions.

A Just Meal

If I settle for your coming and going
would you find a nest in my wings?

Could we share branches,
      twine love,
turn the sharing of worms into a just meal?

Would we plant the tree we land on
in another spot?

Would our kisses be deciduous and lovely?

Merry Go Round

The pony ran off from the carousel and I dreamed of fortunes
through the teabags on my eyes.

I could have been in Central Park.

I don't go too far from home because I like living
        on the same block
where I don't know my neighbors and
I am second cousin to my desires.

I am surrounded by myself and love
now that I know we will die together
in an implosion of togetherness.

Your hands will come out my other side
        and your lips will kiss the back
of my head.

I will walk through you to tomorrow's resilient arrival.

Put on the Map

There is no space so location is guess work.
On the other side of the river there is a land mass before
the next river.

Are we fishing?
Will I lock my hook into your zipper and pull off your dress?

The sadness of your distance is three skips of a rock
across the water.

I get there smooth as a pebble.

You are the environment I put on the map.
You are the snack stand I would open to support you
With the tourists' coins.

I am the car that has broken down before your loveliness.

Foot in My Mouth

I break you like a wishbone and you twist the wish.

There is nothing in the sadness of a snail
except the space in the imbroglio.

I walk through the dunes eating vanilla Carvel.
It melts on my sneakers.

I get on my knees and lick the laces.

I become tongue-tied with my foot in my mouth.
There is a label on my ear that says, "Converse."

In a Couple of Days I Am Flying to Florida

In a couple of days I am flying to Florida.

If a ridiculous underwear or shoe bomber blows
up my plane
I just want the world to know that I don't
forgive them.

That is a form of acquiescence.
That is a way of permitting the unacceptable.
Before I lose consciousness,

falling through the sky like a damaged kite,
I will curse terrorists and their apologists
who didn't weed them out from their midst.

What can you say good about fathers
whose martyred sons are painted on walls?

I Am Nothing

The sun fell down like a reminiscence that
forgot to rise up again into the sky.
That's enough.

I can't write another poem.

I want to disappear into the valley of chocolate
among bonbons.

Let bygones be bygones
and resurrection be a foot up on a new day.

I put a leash around my neck and take myself for a walk.
I have a conversation with a hydrant.
I drink water from a neighbor's pail.

I run back to the pet shop to tell the owner that I don't like
my parents.
My folks smack my nose with a magazine.

I read the headlines and don't see a word about my ambitions.

I am not the President.
I am not the man who became a dog.

Red Wheelbarrow

Suicide is the wrong turn on a confused lane
in an aluminum forest where
the echo is cheap.

I roar like Hamlet.

I will fight until my death like
the prince of Denmark.

Ah, maybe not.

Maybe I am a chicken running around the yard
being chased by William Carlos Williams.

I do not know whether water is falling against
my face or glass.

I look out into the neighbor's yard and
squash my nose.

I want to get out of this place and fill a red
wheelbarrow with matches.

I want to burn the neighbor's house down.

There Is No Healing

People talk about healing after *Charlie Hebdo*.
That's an insult to the dead.
There will be no healing.

Murder is an open wound that repeats itself
in a corner of space
like a permanent invisibility in a missed
opportunity.

How can you heal the dead or the living
who are attached to them?

That's a mere trick to satisfy the survivors and
put gauze over a wound
with the bullet still in it.

Winning and Losing

Time is a thimble that catches blood from a previous scratch.
I am all itchy for love.
I put my hand in a glove and catch an accidental ball.
I play with your intentions like a catcher
putting down fingers at the plate.
We share private communication.
I am so glad that you are on the mound
and the attention is on how we pass secret feelings.
In the audience the crowd is rooting for us to die.
They still have that old gladiatorial spirit.
They don't see that we've moved on to another game.
I like baseball.
Not as a sport but as an indication that scoring matters.
If you can't win the other team can't lose and sometimes
their destructiveness just needs to be put back in the dugout.

Brother

I never write about my brother.
        He's there.
You don't write about the obvious.

I am busy trying to charm
        the subtle
                into having a definition.

Pete,
we never go this way or wander that.

We are just that.

That's the long and the short
of it.
        Brothers till we die

and then some if I can find something
to write about us.

Like the secure being of nothing
        extraordinary.
Like the air that pumps our lungs.

Like friendly arm-wrestles at the center
        of a misplaced locker room that
has been there since we were born.

A Coffee Break

I go downstairs to Starbucks to get an iced coffee grande
and two vanilla scones.
They offer three for the price of two
but I don't like discounts.
You get what you pay for in life
and then you die.
There used to be a salesgirl there who was my friend.
She called me grandpa and gave me free coffee.
I accept gifts.
Free is not a cheap man trying to save a dollar.
Free is the air you breathe when the aftertaste
doesn't remind you that you are separate from it.
I am back in my office trying to write something about
the experience of going to Starbucks
for no reason.
Everything fascinates me.
I can't stop talking about what I see coming and going
and that at sixty-two I am surely going.
I've enjoyed this life like a lemon.
I purse my lips
and suck in the tart misbehavior of my years.
I'd like to send a thank-you note to myself for having been
so daring
but I know I could have done better.
I could have crashed that car at seventeen into a tree and
rode my dashboard to heaven.

After Hearing Dr. Newdow Embarrass My Anthem

Respecting religion like a true atheist,
    I have not been gifted
        with God
    in my pocket
in my heart
in my absentee soul.

Let them have prayers at the inauguration
and at every school
the Ten Commandments at all the courthouses
    and God's praises
        on every dollar bill.

I should not be jealous of God's popularity
    or wish him silenced in our anthems
or hymns.

I am proud that I am alone in the universe
    with no future but dust
        and bone mold.

But I don't resent the faithful's afterlife
or their love of a naked man on a cross.

If only Christ were a woman.
But heck, as Joe E. Brown said in *Some
    Like It Hot*,
"Nobody's perfect."

Ringside at Gleason's Boxing Gym

When I was a young poet skiing on white glaciers
in Oregon
I never thought I would live my life,
my wife-of-a-life,

my sacred-to-me breathing in-
and-out life,
in a boxing gym.

I am missing the boosts of white air and the snow
gargling expectations in
the thin
garrulous lightness of the clouds
mounting
the sun like a hot, humping dog disguised
in vapor.

But I am here in the now and walloped
with no humdrum
but ecstatic punches, delirious hits,
whacking thuds
and the angels of unconsciousness
surrounding me like a breath of hurt, fresh air.

Hope at Gleason's Gym

for Hope Reichbach

Everyone at the gym is telling me that they are sorry that Hope is dead.
They are paying their respects to me as if I am the father.
I know her father.
I am only her trainer.
I am just another tourist in the country of friends' tombstones.
John Douglas wishes that Hope ducked like he taught her when
death entered the ring.
Lennox Blackmore asks me, "Is that little girl of yours dead?"
Hector Roca, who trained me and world champions,
says, "It's so sad. She's like family."
Bruce Silverglade says that she was part of Gleason's gym,
a piece of its history.
She came here at twelve,
one of the early surge of female boxers.
I thought she was too proper to train with me,
too well brought up,
somehow too mature for her age.
She kept coming back for ten years between charity trips
and colleges,
like the gym had something to offer her,
some underbelly of life that she wanted to understand
like a shark stalking dolphins.
You are not one of the world champions who trained here.
You were just another girl who made it seem like the world
was not such a lost, dangerous place
and that grace could flit like Tinker Bell above the croc,
the uppercuts and Captain Hooks in Neverland.

On Georgia O'Keefe's Planet

Everywhere I go I see the skulls of cattle like the paintings
of Georgia O'Keefe.
Death is silent and rushes through the hollow bones
like the wind absent its rush.
It all comes to nothing
even though the ride on the broken-down jeep
was fun.
I open my canteen and drink the sand.
I love my wife like tomorrow
when I am not angry at her like Tuesday.
If you can't find peace in a relationship
you can't find hope
in the impossible.
I watch her hand in mine and wonder if we are picking
at each other or loosening the grip
of each other's arthritis.
There is no one I would have rather walked through
the desert of death with and blown the ram's horn
like a call to religion
like the temple's plot
like the atheist's admission of eternal absence.

ജ്ഞ

Acknowledgments

Antioch Review: "My Tooth"

Aries: "Minor Chords," "The Skate Key"

Ascent: "In an Idle Comment," "Dog Story," "Doing My Own Thing"

Atlanta Review: "Ringside at Gleason's Boxing Gym"

Avocet: "You Got Me Babe"

Awakenings: "Sleeping in Separate Rooms," "I Don't Mind," I Am Not Lunch," "The Kid on the Subway," "A Ski Life"

Barbaric Yawp: "On Stealing Hemingway's Wives"

Bluestem: "Put on the Map"

Caveat Lector: "It's a Wonderful Life," "I Am Nothing"

Chiron Review: "Brain Snatcher"

Chrysalis: "Riding Madison," "A Just Meal"

Clark Street Review: "Accident on Madison Avenue"

Comstock Review: "Foot in My Mouth"

Deronda: "From the Other Side of the Totem Pole," "Grandstanding," "In a Couple Of Days "I Am Flying to Florida," "There Is No Healing"

Edgz: "On Georgia O'Keefe's Planet"

The Electric Muse: "Tennis"

Flint Hills Review: "Nothing"

Four Way Review: "Trees"

Green Hills Literary Lantern: "Ribbons," "In Your Birdcage," "Merry Go Round," "Still Crazy," "Eat Up," "I Am a Tripod"

Harbinger Asylum: "Red Wheelbarrow"

Illuminations: "We," "My Poems"

Iodine: "Elephant Skin Wallet"

The Journal (England): "It's Not Friendship," "A Career Of Sorts"

Listening Eye: "Brother"

Mudrush: "Winning and Losing"

Nth Position: "Thinking About It"

Open Minds: "All My Little Candies," "What We Mean"

Pennsylvania English: "Thinking About You," "Face Painting"

Penwood: "Niagara Falls"

Pinyon: "Can't Get Away"

Plainsongs: "Cuts"

Poetalk: "Dillon"

Queen's Ledger: "Hope at Gleason's Gym"

Skidrow Penthouse: "Strangling a Sherpa"

Straylight: "Reading Your Book"

Stepping Stones Magazine: "Timing"

The Stray Branch: "Spooning," "Green House," "Endless Passage,"
    "One Eyeball"

Stepping Stones Magazine: "Head Bump"

Tatoo Highway: "A Brazen Hug"

Tribeca Poetry Review: "Intentionality," "Letters to No One"

Willard And Maple: "A Coffee Break"

Writer's Bloc: "Leafy Sky"

Writer's Journal: "After Hearing Dr. Newdow Embarrass My Atheism"

About FutureCycle Press

FutureCycle Press is dedicated to publishing lasting English-language poetry books, chapbooks, and anthologies in both print-on-demand and Kindle ebook formats. Founded in 2007 by long-time independent editor/publishers and partners Diane Kistner and Robert S. King, the press incorporated as a nonprofit in 2012. A number of our editors are distinguished poets and writers in their own right, and we have been actively involved in the small press movement going back to the early seventies.

The FutureCycle Poetry Book Prize and honorarium is awarded annually for the best full-length volume of poetry we publish in a calendar year. Introduced in 2013, our Good Works projects are anthologies devoted to issues of universal significance, with all proceeds donated to a related worthy cause. Our Selected Poems series highlights contemporary poets with a substantial body of work to their credit; with this series we strive to resurrect work that has had limited distribution and is now out of print.

We are dedicated to giving all of the authors we publish the care their work deserves, making our catalog of titles the most diverse and distinguished it can be, and paying forward any earnings to fund more great books.

We've learned a few things about independent publishing over the years. We've also evolved a unique, resilient publishing model that allows us to focus mainly on vetting and preserving for posterity poetry collections of exceptional quality without becoming overwhelmed with bookkeeping and mailing, fundraising activities, or taxing editorial and production "bubbles." To find out more about what we are doing, come see us at www.futurecycle.org.

The FutureCycle Poetry Book Prize

All full-length volumes of poetry published by FutureCycle Press in a given calendar year are considered for the annual FutureCycle Poetry Book Prize. This allows us to consider each submission on its own merits, outside of the context of a contest. Too, the judges see the finished book, which will have benefitted from the beautiful book design and strong editorial gloss we are famous for.

The book ranked the best in judging is announced as the prize-winner in the subsequent year. There is no fixed monetary award; instead, the winning poet receives an honorarium of 20% of the total net royalties from all poetry books and chapbooks the press sold online in the year the winning book was published. The winner is also accorded the honor of being on the panel of judges for the next year's competition; all judges receive copies of all contending books to keep for their personal library.

www.ingramcontent.com/pod-product-compliance
Lightning Source LLC
Chambersburg PA
CBHW070009100426
42741CB00012B/3170